BEFORE THE CHAOS

A Practical Planner for Life, Death, and the Mess in Between

Benjamin Cochran, DNP, NP-C

Family Nurse Practitioner & Deputy Coroner

For permission requests, write to: jsp@justsomepodcast.com

This planner is intended for informational purposes only and does not constitute legal or medical advice. Always consult with a qualified professional for any legal, financial, or healthcare decisions.

Printed in the United States of America

Published by Just Some Podcast Media
ISBN: 979-8-9994073-0-6

A Note from Me to You

In chaos theory, there's the idea that something as small as a butterfly flapping its wings can trigger a typhoon halfway around the world. One small shift—unseen, unplanned—can cause a ripple that changes everything.

Life works like that too.

A single diagnosis. A phone call in the middle of the night. A missed piece of paperwork. One small moment can unravel everything you thought was under control.

I've seen it firsthand. As a family nurse practitioner and deputy coroner, I've stood in the chaos. But I've also seen how a little preparation can bring clarity when everything else feels upside down.

This planner isn't about fearing the worst. It's about preparing with purpose. It's about making sure the people you love aren't left guessing. And it's about giving yourself a North Star in the middle of chaos—even if the wings that set it in motion were your own.

Take it one page at a time. Fill in what you can. Let this be your family's steady point in the storm.

—Ben

Table of Contents

Section 1 Setting the Compass

A Note from Me to You

Before you get into the medications, surgeries, or providers, let's talk about *why* this section matters.

When someone ends up in the ER or is facing a health crisis, there's usually one person left digging through drawers, guessing what medications they're on, or trying to remember the name of that specialist they saw once three years ago. That person might be your spouse, your kid, your best friend, or a first responder. This section is for them.

These pages aren't just forms – they're a lifeline. If you're unconscious, unavailable, or just overwhelmed, this is where someone can turn to find clarity. What meds you take. What you're allergic to. Who your providers are. Whether or not you have a medical condition no one else knows about. The details that can make all the difference in stressful moments.

It's also for *you*. Getting all this written down in one place can give you peace of mind and save you time the next time you fill out "one of those forms" at the doctor's office.

You don't have to do it all in one sitting. Start where it's easy. Come back to it when you're ready. You're not filling out paperwork – you're giving your people a map for when things get chaotic.

That's the goal: clarity in the storm.

- Ben

Personal Information

This page captures your basic personal information – legal name, contact details, language, and more. It may seem simple, but in an emergency, having the right spelling of your name or access to your insurance number can save time and avoid confusion. Update as needed if your address, phone, or other details change.

Full Legal Name: _____

Preferred Name/Nickname: _____

Date of Birth:_____

Social Security Number (optional): _____

Address:_____

Phone Number: _____

Email Address: _____

Primary Language: _____

Religion (if applicable): _____

Insurance Information – Since policies and cards can change over time, I recommend keeping a photocopy of the front and back of your current insurance card here. Having this information easily accessible helps avoid delays in care or confusion during emergencies, especially if someone else is trying to advocate for you.

Healthcare Providers & Specialists

This page is for listing the medical providers involved in your care – past or present. From your primary care provider to specialists and therapists, having this information in one place helps your care team, family, or emergency responders reach the right people quickly. Include anyone you think might be helpful in understanding your medical history or current treatment.

Primary Care Provider

Name: _____

Clinic/Facility: _____

Phone: _____

City/State: _____

List specialists that you have or are seeing. The type is for listing what type of provider they are (ex: cardiology).

Specialist Providers

Name	Type	Phone	City/State

Medication Information

This section is for recording important information about your medications. Use it to list prescriptions, over-the-counter meds, supplements, preferred pharmacies, and any known allergies. If a medication is stopped or discontinued, simply mark through it with a single line (ex: ~~lisinopril~~) – don't erase it. Keeping a record of changes can be just as helpful as knowing what you're currently taking.

Allergies	Reaction
Ex: Penicillin	Rash
_____	_____
_____	_____
_____	_____
_____	_____
_____	_____
_____	_____

If you need more space for allergies, please feel free to photocopy and include a list in this section.

Preferred Pharmacy: _____

Secondary Pharmacy (if applicable): _____

If there are any special instructions for pharmacies, please jot that down here. Some medications may need to be filled locally while others go through mail order – note any preferences below.

Notes:

_____

_____

Medication Information (continued)

Medication	Dosage	Directions	Reason

Medication Information (continued)

Medication	Dosage	Directions	Reason

Medication Information

Past Medical History

This is where you document the big-picture health stuff – chronic conditions, major diagnoses, and anything that helps someone understand your overall medical story. Include the year or age at diagnosis if possible. This info gives providers and caregivers context that could influence treatment decisions in the future. Please include things like physical (like hypertension) or mental (like anxiety). Include conditions for which you take medications in this section. If a condition has resolved, mark through it with a single line (ex. ~~Hypertension~~).

Condition	Year/Age of Diagnosis	Condition	Year/Age of Diagnosis

Past Surgical History

Use this space to list any surgeries or major procedures you've had. Include the type of surgery and the month and year, if you remember it. If not, just the year is fine. Even older procedures can be relevant, especially if you're undergoing future treatment or imaging

Surgery	Month/Year
Ex: Gallbladder	Sept 2018

Past Surgical History (continued)

Surgery	Month/Year

Family Medical History

This section helps you track chronic or hereditary conditions that run in your family. Just check the boxes next to the relatives who had the condition. Family history can play a major role in how healthcare providers assess your risk for certain illnesses, so the more detail you include, the more useful it becomes.

Condition	Relation
Ex: Hypertension	☐ Mother ☐ Father ☐ Uncle ☐ Aunt ☐ Brother ☐ Sister ☐ Paternal Grandma ☐ Paternal Grandpa ☐ Maternal Grandma ☐ Maternal Grandpa ☐ Other _____
	☐ Mother ☐ Father ☐ Uncle ☐ Aunt ☐ Brother ☐ Sister ☐ Paternal Grandma ☐ Paternal Grandpa ☐ Maternal Grandma ☐ Maternal Grandpa ☐ Other _____
	☐ Mother ☐ Father ☐ Uncle ☐ Aunt ☐ Brother ☐ Sister ☐ Paternal Grandma ☐ Paternal Grandpa ☐ Maternal Grandma ☐ Maternal Grandpa ☐ Other _____
	☐ Mother ☐ Father ☐ Uncle ☐ Aunt ☐ Brother ☐ Sister ☐ Paternal Grandma ☐ Paternal Grandpa ☐ Maternal Grandma ☐ Maternal Grandpa ☐ Other _____
	☐ Mother ☐ Father ☐ Uncle ☐ Aunt ☐ Brother ☐ Sister ☐ Paternal Grandma ☐ Paternal Grandpa ☐ Maternal Grandma ☐ Maternal Grandpa ☐ Other _____
	☐ Mother ☐ Father ☐ Uncle ☐ Aunt ☐ Brother ☐ Sister ☐ Paternal Grandma ☐ Paternal Grandpa ☐ Maternal Grandma ☐ Maternal Grandpa ☐ Other _____
	☐ Mother ☐ Father ☐ Uncle ☐ Aunt ☐ Brother ☐ Sister ☐ Paternal Grandma ☐ Paternal Grandpa ☐ Maternal Grandma ☐ Maternal Grandpa ☐ Other _____
	☐ Mother ☐ Father ☐ Uncle ☐ Aunt ☐ Brother ☐ Sister ☐ Paternal Grandma ☐ Paternal Grandpa ☐ Maternal Grandma ☐ Maternal Grandpa ☐ Other _____

Family Medical History (continued)

Condition	Relation
	☐ Mother ☐ Father ☐ Uncle ☐ Aunt ☐ Brother ☐ Sister ☐ Paternal Grandma ☐ Paternal Grandpa ☐ Maternal Grandma ☐ Maternal Grandpa ☐ Other _____
	☐ Mother ☐ Father ☐ Uncle ☐ Aunt ☐ Brother ☐ Sister ☐ Paternal Grandma ☐ Paternal Grandpa ☐ Maternal Grandma ☐ Maternal Grandpa ☐ Other _____
	☐ Mother ☐ Father ☐ Uncle ☐ Aunt ☐ Brother ☐ Sister ☐ Paternal Grandma ☐ Paternal Grandpa ☐ Maternal Grandma ☐ Maternal Grandpa ☐ Other _____
	☐ Mother ☐ Father ☐ Uncle ☐ Aunt ☐ Brother ☐ Sister ☐ Paternal Grandma ☐ Paternal Grandpa ☐ Maternal Grandma ☐ Maternal Grandpa ☐ Other _____
	☐ Mother ☐ Father ☐ Uncle ☐ Aunt ☐ Brother ☐ Sister ☐ Paternal Grandma ☐ Paternal Grandpa ☐ Maternal Grandma ☐ Maternal Grandpa ☐ Other _____
	☐ Mother ☐ Father ☐ Uncle ☐ Aunt ☐ Brother ☐ Sister ☐ Paternal Grandma ☐ Paternal Grandpa ☐ Maternal Grandma ☐ Maternal Grandpa ☐ Other _____
	☐ Mother ☐ Father ☐ Uncle ☐ Aunt ☐ Brother ☐ Sister ☐ Paternal Grandma ☐ Paternal Grandpa ☐ Maternal Grandma ☐ Maternal Grandpa ☐ Other _____
	☐ Mother ☐ Father ☐ Uncle ☐ Aunt ☐ Brother ☐ Sister ☐ Paternal Grandma ☐ Paternal Grandpa ☐ Maternal Grandma ☐ Maternal Grandpa ☐ Other _____
	☐ Mother ☐ Father ☐ Uncle ☐ Aunt ☐ Brother ☐ Sister ☐ Paternal Grandma ☐ Paternal Grandpa ☐ Maternal Grandma ☐ Maternal Grandpa ☐ Other _____

Things I Want My Providers to Know

This is the stuff that doesn't always make it into a chart – but it matters. Maybe it's a medication that didn't sit right with you but wasn't technically an allergy. Maybe you have a hard time with needles, or certain procedures bring up bad memories.

Use it to jot down anything that could help your provider understand *you* – not just your labs or diagnoses. These details might feel small, but in the middle of a stressful moment, they can help your care feel more human, more respectful, and more in tune with what you need.

No wrong answers. No judgment. Just you, being honest, in your own words.

_____

_____

_____

_____

_____

_____

_____

HEADS UP ON LEGAL DOCUMENTS

If you have completed an Advanced Directive or named a healthcare power of attorney, keep a copy in this planner and let your provider know where it's located.

You can download your state's official forms at www.justsomepodcast.com/directives (English and Spanish versions available).
Forms provided by the National Hospice and Palliative Care Organization

16

Section 2 Middle of The Map

A Note from Me to You

There comes a point where the road ahead isn't as clear as it used to be. You're not at the end, but you can feel the shift. Maybe it's a diagnosis. Maybe it's age or it's just that gut feeling that it's time to get things in order. This part of the planner is about being ready for that shift – before the pressure and chaos hit.

Advance directives, powers of attorney, living wills – this isn't just paperwork. It's peace of mind. It's your voice on paper when you can't speak for yourself. It's a way to protect your family from the weight of hard choices, especially when emotions are high and time is short.

I've seen too many families struggle because these conversations never happened. I've seen the guilt, the confusion, and the chaos that fills the silence when someone's wishes aren't known. But I've also seen the calm that comes when everything's clear – when there's a plan, and everyone knows where it came from.

So, use this section to lay it all out. Be clear and be honest. Let it reflect who you are and what matters to you. You're not lost – you're just in the middle of the map. Feel free to take your time and think about this section. This is your chance to voice your wishes when you are no longer able to do so.

Let this section be your family's North Star – steady, visible, and guiding them when the storm rolls in.

- Ben

What You Should Know

What is a Durable Power of Attorney for Healthcare (DPOA-HC)?

It's a legal form that lets you name someone to make healthcare decisions if you can't. That could be because you're unconscious, confused, heavily medicated, or simply too sick to speak for yourself. This person becomes your voice – and they're legally allowed to speak on your behalf.

Why do I need one?

Because medical emergencies don't come with a warning. And in those moments, your doctors need to know who's in charge of making the call. If you don't have this set up, your family might be forced to go to court or argue with each other while you're lying in a hospital bed. This avoids all that.

When does it go into effect?

Only if you can't make your own medical decisions. As long as you're awake, alert, and able to speak for yourself, you stay in control. This just kicks in if you're too out of it to say what you want.

Who should I choose?

Pick someone who knows you well, can stay calm under pressure, and will follow your wishes – even if others don't agree. It doesn't have to be your spouse or oldest child. It should be the person who will advocate for you, ask the right questions, and stand firm if needed.

Can I change it later?

Absolutely. You can update or cancel it at any time – as long as you're mentally capable. Life changes, and so can your decisions.

What kinds of decisions can they make?
They can approve or refuse treatments, choose hospitals or doctors, speak to your care team, and access your medical records. If it's a medical decision, they're the one in the driver's seat.

Should I talk to the person I'm naming?
Yes, yes, yes. They need to know you've chosen them – and they need to feel ready to take that on. Tell them what matters most to you. Don't assume they'll just "know what you want."

Is this the same as a financial power of attorney?
Nope. That's a separate document. The healthcare DPOA only covers medical decisions. If you want someone to manage money or bills, that's a different section.

The next few pages have a Durable Power of Attorney that can be filled out and used or you can download and print forms from the website listed below. If you already have one, feel free to photocopy it and keep it in this section.

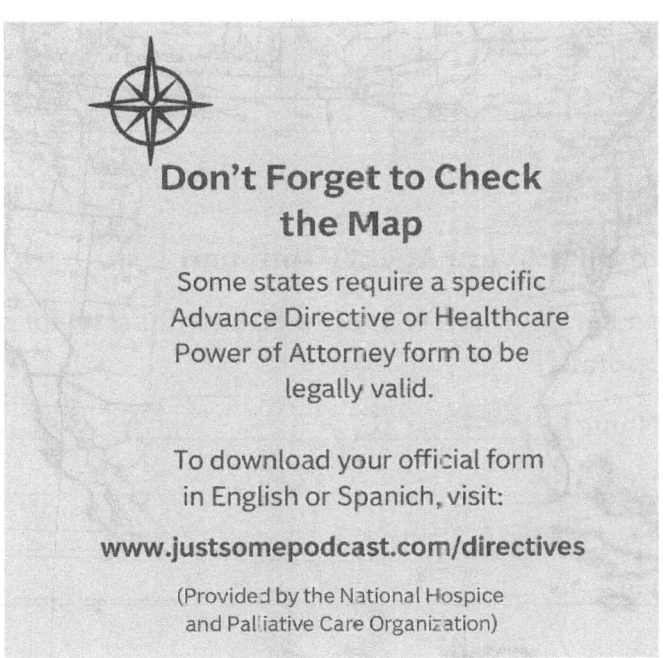

**Don't Forget to Check
the Map**

Some states require a specific
Advance Directive or Healthcare
Power of Attorney form to be
legally valid.

To download your official form
in English or Spanish, visit:

www.justsomepodcast.com/directives

(Provided by the National Hospice
and Palliative Care Organization)

Durable Power of Attorney for Healthcare

This form allows you to appoint someone you trust to make medical decisions for you if you become unable to make them yourself.

1. Your Information (Principal)

Full Legal Name: _____

Date of Birth: _____

2. Primary Healthcare Agent (DPOA-HC)

I appoint the following person as my healthcare decision-maker:

(Agent may not be the treating healthcare provider, an employee of the treating healthcare provider, or an employee, owner, director or officer of a facility, unless that person is a relative or is bound to you by common vows)

Full Legal Name: _____

Relationship: _____

Address: _____

Phone: _____

Email: _____

3. Alternate Healthcare Agent (Optional)

If the person listed above is unable or unwilling to act on my behalf, I appoint:

Full Legal Name: _____

Relationship: _____

Address: _____

Phone: _____

Email: _____

4. Scope of Authority

My healthcare agent is authorized to make decisions about my medical care, including but not limited to:

- Accessing and sharing my medical records
- Approving or refusing medical treatments
- Making decisions about life-sustaining care, surgery, or hospitalization
- Choosing healthcare providers or facilities
- Authorizing pain management, palliative, or hospice care
- Making decisions based on my known wishes or, if unknown, in my best interest

My healthcare agent may not:

- Exceed the powers set out in writing in this document
- Revoke any existing Living Will declaration I may have

Initial here to confirm: _____

6. Duration

This power of attorney remains in effect:

- Until I revoke it in writing
- Indefinitely unless I state otherwise below:

7. Signature

This power of attorney for healthcare decisions shall become effective when I am unable to make decisions or unable to communicate my wishes regarding healthcare. This power of attorney for health care decisions shall become effective upon the disability or incapacity of the principal. Any durable power of attorney for healthcare decisions I have made previously is hereby revoked.

If I have an advance directive, my advance directive controls and take precedence over this power of attorney.

By signing below, I affirm that I understand this document and voluntarily appoint the healthcare agent(s) listed above.

Signature: _____

Printed Name: _____

Date: _____

8. Witness or Notary

Some states require a notary. Some require two witnesses. There is a table in the appendix that lists each state's requirements (as of the printing of this book).

Option A: Witnesses

I declare that the principal signed this document willingly and appeared to be of sound mind. I am not the named agent or related to the principal.

Witness #1:	**Witness #2:**
Signature: _____	_____
Printed Name: _____	_____
Date: _____	_____

Option B: Notary Public

State of _____ County of _____   Notary Seal:

Subscribed and sworn before me on
this _____ day of _____, **20**___

Notary Public Signature: _____
My commission expires: _____

22

Advance Directives

What You Should Know About Advance Directives

An **Advance Directive** is a legal document that tells your healthcare providers what kind of care you do you don't want if you can't speak for yourself.

Think of it like a medical game plan. If you're unconscious, confused, or too sick to decide, this is the document that helps guide your care.

Advance Directives often cover things like:

- Whether you want to be kept alive by machines
- If you want CPR or not
- Your thoughts on feeding tubes or dialysis
- Whether comfort care (palliative or hospice) is more important than aggressive treatment

You can be specific, or you can keep it simple. The goal is to give clear direction, based on *your* values – not what someone else assumes you'd want.

This form works hand-in-hand with your **Healthcare Power of Attorney** (the person you named to speak for you). It doesn't replace that person – it just gives them a guide to follow. An Advanced Directive can control and take precedence over your DPOA.

You can change your Advance Directive anytime. Just make sure the most recent version is shared with your healthcare team, your proxy, and your family.

⚠ *Before You Fill This Out*

Take a few minutes to read through the full form before you start making selections. Some of the terms like "life-sustaining treatments" or "comfort care" may not mean what you think at first glance.

Each section includes plain-language explanations to help you understand what those treatments actually involve. There's nc rush. This is about making decisions that reflect your values, not just checking a box.

23

Advance Directive for Healthcare

This document allows you to state your medical care preferences in case you become unable to speak for yourself. It also serves as a guide for your healthcare proxy or care team.

1. Your Information (Principal)

Full Legal Name: _____

Date of Birth: _____

2. Statement of Intent

If I am unable to make my own medical decisions due to illness, injury, or incapacity, I want my healthcare providers and the person(s) I've designated as my healthcare power of attorney to follow the directions I've outlined in this form.

3. Life-Sustaining Treatments

Please check **ONE** option below:

☐ **I want all possible life-sustaining treatments.**
This includes CPR, ventilators, dialysis, artificial nutrition/hydration, and other intensive medical interventions.

☐ **I want life-sustaining treatments only if they are likely to help me recover.**
If there's little chance of recovery or meaningful quality of life, I do *not* want aggressive measures.

☐ **I do NOT want life-sustaining treatments if I am near death or permanently unconscious.**
I prefer comfort-focused care only.

4. Specific Preferences

(Initial next to each that applies, and feel free to add notes.)

_____ **CPR (Cardiopulmonary Resuscitation):** Attempt to restart my heart if it stops.

☐ Yes ☐ No

_____ **Mechanical Ventilation (Breathing Machines):** Used if I can't breathe on my own.

☐ Yes ☐ No ☐ Only short-term

_____ **Artificial Nutrition & Hydration (Feeding Tubes/IV Fluids):**

☐ Yes ☐ No ☐ Only if temporary

_____ **Dialysis:** Used to clean the blood if kidneys fail.

☐ Yes ☐ No

_____ **Pain Management:** Always provide pain relief and comfort measures, even if it may shorten life.

☐ Yes ☐ No

_____ **Hospice or Palliative Care:** Focus on comfort, dignity, and quality of life rather than cure.

☐ Yes ☐ No

---

5. Organ and Tissue Donation

☐ I do **not** wish to donate my organs or tissues.

☐ I **do** wish to donate my organs and/or tissues for transplant, research, or education.

---

6. Religious or Personal Beliefs to Consider

If there are spiritual or cultural beliefs that should guide my care, please describe them here:

7. Signature and Date

I declare that I am of sound mind and making this directive voluntarily.

Signature: _____

Printed Name: _____

Date: _____

8. Witness or Notary

Some states require a notary. Some require two witnesses. There is a table in the appendix that lists each state's requirements (as of the printing of this book).

Option A: Witnesses

I declare that the principal signed this document willingly and appeared to be of sound mind. I am not the DPOA or related to the principal.

	Witness #1:	**Witness #2:**
Signature:	_____	_____
Printed Name:	_____	_____
Date:	_____	_____

Option B: Notary Public

State of _____ County of _____   Notary Seal:

Subscribed and sworn before me on
this _____ day of _____, **20___**

Notary Public Signature: _____

My commission expires: _____

Psychiatric Advance Directive

What You Should Know

A **Mental Health Directive** (also called a Psychiatric Advance Directive or PAD) lets you state your preferences for mental health treatment **before a crisis happens** when you're clear-headed, stable, and able to make informed decisions.

It helps your healthcare providers and loved ones understand:

- What medications work well for you (or which ones don't)
- What hospitals or providers you prefer
- Who you want to be involved—or not involved—in your care
- How you want to be treated if you're experiencing a mental health crisis

If you've ever been through psychiatric care, or you're managing a mental health condition, this document gives you the power to guide your treatment when you might not be able to speak clearly for yourself.

Even if you've never had a mental health crisis, this is still a helpful way to make sure your values and boundaries are respected.

Psychiatric Advanced Directive

1. Your Information (Principal)

Full Legal Name: _____

Date of Birth: _____

2. Mental Health Conditions (if any): List any diagnoses or conditions you'd like providers to be aware of (optional):

_____

_____

3. Medications That Work Well for Me: List names, doses, or brands you've responded well to in the past.

_____

_____

4. Medications I Do NOT Want: Include those that caused side effects, made you worse, or you wish to avoid.

_____

_____

5. Preferred Mental Health Providers or Facilities: If there's a clinic, provider, or hospital you trust – or places you want to avoid you can list them here.

Preferred: _____

Avoid if possible: _____

6. Treatment Preferences: Initial any that apply and feel free to add notes:

_____ **I prefer to receive care at home if possible**

_____ **I consent to voluntary hospitalization if needed**

_____ **I do not consent to involuntary hospitalization unless required by law**

_____ **I do NOT want restraints or seclusion unless absolutely necessary**

_____ **I prefer a family member or friend be contacted before medication changes**

_____ **I consent to electroconvulsive therapy (ECT) if recommended**

Notes:

_____

_____

7. People I Want Involved in My Mental Health Care

Name: _____   Name: _____
Relationship: _____   Relationship: _____
Phone: _____   Phone: _____
☐ Share full info with them   ☐ Share full info with them
☐ Only contact in emergency   ☐ Only contact in emergency

8. People I Do NOT Want Involved

Name: _____   Name: _____

Relationship: _____   Relationship: _____

(Optional)

Reason: _____   Reason: _____

9. Signature & Date

I am of sound mind and completing this document voluntarily to guide my mental health care if I become unable to make decisions or communicate clearly.

Signature: _____

Date: _____

10. Witness or Notary (Optional but Recommended)

Follow your state's requirements for mental health directives. Some may require notarization or witness signatures for legal recognition. A table of state requirements (as of this printing) is listed in the appendix or can be found at www.justsomepodcast.com/directives.

Option A: Witnesses

I declare that the principal signed this document willingly and appeared to be of sound mind. I am not the DPOA or related to the principal.

Witness #1:	**Witness #2:**
Signature: _____	_____
Printed Name: _____	_____
Date: _____	_____

Option B: Notary Public

State of _____ County of _____   Notary Seal:

Subscribed and sworn before me on this _____ day of _____, **20___**

Notary Public Signature: _____

My commission expires: _____

HIPAA Authorization

What You Should Know About HIPAA Authorization

HIPAA stands for the **Health Insurance Portability and Accountability Act**. It's a federal law that protects your private health information from being shared without your permission.

That's usually a good thing.
But in a medical emergency, it can also leave the people who care about you stuck on the outside looking in.

Without your explicit consent, doctors and hospitals **cannot legally talk** to your spouse, partner, children, best friend, or even your healthcare power of attorney about your condition. Not your diagnosis. Not your test results. Not what room you're in. Nothing.

This form called a **HIPAA Authorization** fixes that.

It lets you list who can be told what's going on with you if you're sick, injured, or unable to speak for yourself. You can choose to give:

- Full access to everything in your medical records
- Access only to specific types of information (like labs, billing, or mental health)
- Permission for someone to get updates, but not make any decisions on your behalf

This is **not** a power of attorney form. It doesn't give anyone control over your care or money. It just opens the door so your people aren't left guessing or being told "Sorry, we can't give out that information."

You can change or revoke this form at any time. You're still in control.

If you've got someone you trust to support you through a health crisis, give them the tools to actually *help you* starting with this form.

31

Is this form legally valid?

*Yes. This form includes everything required under **federal HIPAA law** **(45 CFR § 164.508)**. It's legally valid in **all 50 states and U.S. territories**.*

Will every hospital accept it?

Most will. Some may still ask you to sign their in-house version too – but this form is still valid and a great starting point, especially in emergencies.

HIPAA Authorization for Release of Medical Information

1. Your Information (Patient)

Full Legal Name: _____

Date of Birth: _____

Address: _____

2. Persons Authorized to Receive Information

I authorize the following individuals to access my medical records and communicate with my healthcare providers as permitted under HIPAA:

Name: _____

Phone: _____

☐ Full Access ☐ Limited (specify): _____

Name: _____

Phone: _____

☐ Full Access ☐ Limited (specify): _____

32

3. Types of Information Authorized (check all that apply)

☐ All medical information, including diagnosis and treatment

☐ Billing and insurance records ☐ Mental health information

☐ Substance use disorder records ☐ Lab results, imaging, and reports ☐ Other (specify): _____

4. Purpose of Disclosure

☐ Continuity of care / emergency support ☐ Legal / financial planning ☐ Personal recordkeeping

☐ Other (optional): _____

5. Expiration of Authorization

This authorization remains valid:

☐ Until I revoke it in writing ☐ Until this date: _____

☐ For the duration of my current treatment or hospitalization

6. Right to Revoke

I understand that I can revoke this authorization at any time by submitting a written notice to my healthcare provider. Revocation does not apply to information already released.

7. Signature and Date

Signature: _____

Date: _____

Care Preferences and Visitation Instructions

What You Should Know

This section is about how you want to be cared for when your health starts to decline – physically, emotionally, and spiritually. It's where you can share what matters most to you when things get serious. Maybe it's staying at home or it's avoiding aggressive treatment. Maybe it's just knowing who you want (or don't want) around you.

These choices aren't about giving someone legal authority. They're about making sure your care still reflects *you*, even when you can't say it out loud.

You don't have to fill out every box. Just write down what feels important. This is about comfort, dignity, and helping your people show up the way you need them to.

Care Preferences and Visitation Instructions

Where I Prefer to Receive Care (Check all that apply)

☐ At home, if possible

☐ In a hospital setting

☐ In a skilled nursing facility

☐ In hospice care (home or facility)

☐ Wherever my medical team recommends based on my condition

☐ Other: _____

Notes (optional):

_____

_____

If My Condition Becomes Terminal or I Am Actively Dying, I Would Prefer...

☐ To remain in familiar surroundings

☐ To be kept comfortable, not treated aggressively

☐ To have music or soft sounds nearby

☐ To have someone physically present with me

☐ To be alone unless I request company

☐ To have spiritual care available (e.g. clergy, rituals)

☐ Other: _____

Notes or Specific Requests:

_____

_____

People I Want Present During a Serious Illness or End-of-Life Care

These are the people I'd want notified and are welcome, especially if I can no longer communicate.

Name	Relationship	Phone	Optional Notes

People I Prefer Not Be Present

You can list anyone you would prefer not be involved in your care or bedside visits. These are not legal restrictions but help your care team understand your wishes.

Name	Relationship	Optional Notes

Other Boundaries, Requests, or Preferences

Use this space for anything that helps you feel respected, safe, or understood during a vulnerable time.

Examples:

- "Please don't post updates on social media."
- "I'd like my pet to visit if possible."
- "Limit noise and bright lights."
- "Allow prayer or meditation, but don't push religion."
- "Keep certain family members apart in the room."

_____

_____

_____

_____

_____

_____

_____

What You Should Know

Planning for what happens after you're gone doesn't just mean saying who gets what. It also means deciding **how** that plan gets carried out and that's where Wills and Trusts come in.

Most people have heard of a Will, and some have heard of a Trust but very few actually understand what they do, how they work, or why it matters which one you use. This page isn't legal advice. It's here to help you make sense of your options and avoid surprises.

Will (Last Will and Testament)

What it does:
- Names who should get your property and assets when you die
- Can name a guardian for minor children
- Names an executor to handle your estate

When it takes effect:
- **Only after you die**
- Has to go through **probate** (a legal process that can take weeks to months)

Good for:
- Simple estates
- People without a lot of assets or minor children
- Having at least *something* in writing if nothing else is in place

---

Trust (Revocable Living Trust)

What it does:
- Lets you move your assets into a legal entity (the trust) while you're still alive
- You still control everything while you're alive

- After you die, your assets go directly to the people you've named - **no probate**

When it takes effect:
- **Immediately** once created and funded
- Can manage your assets if you become incapacitated (before death)

Good for:
- Potentially avoiding court
- Protecting privacy (trusts are not public record)
- Complex estates or blended families
- Planning for long-term care or disability. Of note, long-term care or disability can be extremely complex from a financial perspective. If this is a concern, I highly recommend visiting with an estate planning attorney.

Key Differences at a Glance

Feature	Will	Trust
Goes into effect	After death	Immediately (if funded)
Probate required	Yes	No
Names guardians	Yes	No
Controls assets before death	No	Yes
Public record?	Yes	No
Complex estate planning	Limited	Excellent

What This Means for You

- If you have young kids, a Will is critical to name a guardian.
- If you have a house, a Trust can help your heirs avoid probate.
- If you have both? You're covering your bases. Many people have **both a Will and a Trust.**

39

Even if you're not ready to set up a Trust now, understanding how it works can help you decide what kind of planning is best for your family and your situation.

How to Set Up a Will or Trust (Without Losing Your Mind)

You don't need to be rich to have a Will or a Trust – you just need a plan. Here's how to get started with either one, even if you've never done this before.

To Set Up a Will:

- **Decide what you want to happen.**
  Who gets what? Who should be in charge (executor)? Who would care for minor kids?
- **Choose how to write it:**
    o You can write it by hand (holographic will), but it may not be valid in all states
    o You can use online tools like FreeWill, Trust & Will, or legal software
    o Or you can go through an estate planning attorney **(recommended)**
- **Sign it with witnesses.**
  Most states require two witnesses (not beneficiaries). Some may also allow notarization.
- **Store it safely.**
  Keep the original in a fireproof safe or with a trusted person. Make sure your proxy or executor knows where it is.

To Set Up a Trust:

- **Meet with an estate attorney.**
  Trusts are more complex, so this is where professional help pays off. You'll discuss what you want the trust to do—distribute assets, protect minor kids, avoid probate, manage long-term care, etc.

40

- **Decide who's involved:**
  - **Trustee** – the person managing the trust (can be you at first)
  - **Beneficiaries** – who receives the assets
  - **Successor trustee** – who takes over when you pass or if you become incapacitated
- **Transfer ownership of assets into the trust.**
  This is called "funding" the trust. You'll change the titles on real estate, bank accounts, etc., to be owned by the trust.
- **Maintain it.**
  You can amend a revocable trust at any time. Just be sure to keep it updated if you buy property, open accounts, or change your wishes.

One Last Thing

Even a **simple Will is better than no plan at all**. You don't need to have it all figured out – you just need to get started.

If you're not sure what's right for you, talk to an estate planning attorney or your financial advisor. They'll help guide you based on your specific situation.

Next Steps: Start Planning Your Will or Trust

☐ **Make a list of what you own.**
(Include your house, vehicles, bank accounts, retirement, life insurance, valuables.)

☐ **Think about who gets what and who handles things.**
Who would you trust to manage your estate? Who would take care of your kids?

☐ **Decide if you need just a Will, or a Trust too.**
(If you have a house or want to avoid probate, a Trust may be a good idea.)

☐ **Choose how to get started:**

- ☐ Talk to an estate planning attorney
- ☐ Use a reputable online tool (like Trust & Will, FreeWill, or LegalZoom)
- ☐ Ask your financial advisor if they offer estate planning support

☐ **Write it down, sign it properly.**

(2 witnesses required in most states. Notarization may also help.)

☐ **Tell someone where it's kept.**

(Executor, spouse, or adult child – don't let it disappear in a file drawer.)

☐ **Review and update it every few years.**

Especially after big life events (marriage, divorce, new baby, buying a house, etc.)

Letter to My Healthcare Proxy

What You Should Know

This letter isn't about legal boxes or medical terms. It's about trust.

You chose someone to speak for you when you can't and that's not a small thing. This is your chance to tell them why. Not just what to do, but what matters. What you hope they'll remember when things get hard. What you want them to carry with them when you're quiet and the decisions are heavy.

This doesn't need to be fancy. It just needs to be honest. You can talk about what you value, what you fear, or what would bring you peace when things feel upside down.

The person reading this may be exhausted, scared, or doubting themselves. Give them what they'll need in that moment – your voice, your encouragement, and the reminder that they're not alone in this.

You picked them for a reason. Let them hear it from you.

Letter Template

To: _____

Why I chose you:

_____

_____

_____

_____

_____

What I hope you'll remember if things get hard:

_____

_____

_____

_____

_____

With all my trust,

Date: _____

You don't have to be perfect. Just be present. That's more than enough.

Section 3 Where the Map Fades

A Note from Me to You

This is the section no one wants to think about and the one your family will need the most.

When someone dies, everything changes. Emotions run high and grief can show up in strange ways. But in the middle of all that, there's still paperwork to handle, decisions to make, and people asking questions no one's ready to answer.

That's why this section exists.

Not to be morbid or dramatic. But to give your people something solid to hold onto when everything else feels like it's coming apart.

This is where you write down the things you'd want someone to know after you're gone. The things that could get forgotten. The passwords, the policies, the burial wishes. The accounts that keep charging monthly because no one knew they existed. The military records needed for benefits. The people to call. The ones not to.

This is where you say, *"I took care of it so you don't have to figure it out in the dark."*

Every detail you fill out here is a weight lifted. A moment of clarity in the chaos. A gift of time, peace, and direction for the people who will miss you most.

You don't have to do it all today. But every blank you fill in is one more moment you've made easier for someone else.

Even after the map fades, you can still help them find their way.

- Ben

A Word About Security

This section deals with some of the most sensitive parts of your life: accounts, assets, passwords, financial information, final wishes.

It's meant to **give direction**, not to hand out full access.

To protect yourself (and your family), ***do not*** list:
- Full account numbers
- Full passwords
- Social Security Numbers
- PINs

Instead, use this section to point to where important documents, logins, or information can be found like a secure file, password manager, safe, or trusted person.

If you have many accounts, assets, or important files, it's perfectly fine to use a separate sheet or digital backup. Just be clear about where that information lives.

The goal here isn't to share every detail.
It's to leave a map—not the keys to the vault.

After Death Checklist: What Needs to Happen and When

What You Should Know

When someone dies, there's a moment when grief and logistics collide. The to-do list doesn't wait for anyone to be emotionally ready.

This checklist is here to help with that.

It's broken down by time not because you have to follow it like a script, but because certain things really do need to happen sooner than others. Some steps are legal. Some are practical. Some are just about making sure the person is honored the way they deserve.

Use this list as a guide. Check off what's done, skip what doesn't apply, and come back to it as needed. If you're here, someone trusted you with this part. This is how you show up for them; one step at a time.

The list is in the next few pages, followed by a short notes section if needed.

After Death Checklist

Immediately (Within a Few Hours)

- ☐ **Get legal confirmation of death** (by a doctor, hospice nurse, coroner, or ER)
- ☐ **Arrange transport of the body** to a funeral home or crematorium.
- ☐ **Notify close family or friends**
- ☐ **Look for Advance Directives or DNR orders** if not already in place
- ☐ **Secure pets and dependents**
- ☐ **Begin preserving valuables and property** (lock doors, secure personal items)

Within the First Few Days

- ☐ **Contact funeral home or crematorium** to plan arrangements
- ☐ **Notify the person's primary care provider and/or specialists**
- ☐ **Review the person's will or estate documents**
- ☐ **Contact religious, cultural, or spiritual leaders (if applicable).** Often, funeral home can do this after you meet with them.
- ☐ **Order multiple certified copies of the death certificate** (2-6 recommended depending on assets). This can often be done through the funeral home or crematorium.
- ☐ **Inform employer or former employer** (for life insurance, final pay, benefits)
- ☐ **Notify Social Security Administration** (1-800-772-1213 or online). Typically done by the funeral home automatically via the death certificate. Find out from them if this is something that you need to do.

- ☐ **Begin obituary drafting and distribution (if desired).** The funeral home will likely work with you on this.
- ☐ **Arrange care for surviving dependents or adults with special needs**
- ☐ **If the person served in the military, locate their DD-214.**
  - ○ Needed to request military honors, burial at a national cemetery, U.S. flag, and headstone or marker.

Within 1–2 Weeks

- ☐ **Meet with estate attorney or executor**
- ☐ **File the will with probate court (if required)**
- ☐ **Notify financial institutions** (banks, credit unions, investment firms)
- ☐ **Cancel or transfer utilities, phone, and subscriptions**
- ☐ **Cancel driver's license and voter registration**
- ☐ **Begin gathering and securing assets**
- ☐ **Remove or update access to digital accounts and devices**
- ☐ **Submit life insurance claims**. Start this as soon as possible as this process could take months depending on the death certificate.

Within 1–2 Months

- ☐ **Settle outstanding debts and final bills**
- ☐ **Close or transfer ownership of bank accounts**
- ☐ **Distribute personal property per the will or trust**
- ☐ **Contact credit bureaus to prevent identity theft** (Experian, Equifax, TransUnion)
- ☐ **Update estate tax filings, if applicable**

- ☐ **Work with Social Security or VA if survivor benefits apply**
- ☐ **Change title/ownership for vehicles, home, or land**

Optional Additions

- ☐ **Host a memorial or celebration of life** (if delayed)
- ☐ **Create a memory book or legacy project for children/grandchildren**
- ☐ **Grieve. Seriously. Don't forget to take care of yourself too.**

Notes if need to keep track of things while working through the list.

_____

_____

_____

_____

_____

_____

_____

_____

_____

_____

Final Arrangements

What You Should Know

Planning your final arrangements isn't about being morbid. It's about being kind.

This is the section that helps your family breathe just a little easier on one of the worst days of their lives. It keeps them from having to make hard decisions in a fog of grief. Decisions like "Would they want cremation or burial?" or "Do we need to choose a casket today?" or "Where would they want the service?"

If you've ever sat in a funeral home trying to answer those questions, you already know how heavy that moment can feel. When nothing's written down, it becomes guesswork and guesswork turns into second-guessing, guilt, and sometimes even family conflict.

Whether you want a full traditional funeral, a celebration of life with your favorite playlist, or just a quiet cremation and no fuss at all – you can say that here. You don't need a lawyer. You don't have to prepay or get everything perfect. You just have to write it down.

And if you've already made arrangements with a funeral home or signed up for body donation – great. There's a spot for that too.

Even if you're not sure yet, start with what feels right. Do you want to be buried in a certain place? Scattered somewhere meaningful? Do you care who speaks at your memorial or whether there is one at all?

Write it in your words. Fill out what you can. Cross out what doesn't fit.

This isn't about controlling the moment. It's about giving your people peace, direction, and the chance to honor you the way you'd want without wondering if they got it wrong.

Final Arrangements/Funeral Planning

Funeral Home Preference: _____

If you have preferences for your final wishes, it would be highly recommended to visit with the funeral home listed above to discuss these wishes. Often, they can help guide your wishes and assist with decisions that could save your family lots of hard decisions.

Disposition Preference (check one)

☐ Burial

☐ Cremation

☐ Donation to science (has to be preapproved in most cases)

☐ I've already made arrangements (see below)

☐ Other: _____

If Burial:

- Preferred Cemetery: _____
- Plot already purchased? ☐ Yes ☐ No If yes, under what name? _____
- Casket preferences: _____
- Clothing or items I'd like buried with me:

If Cremation:

- Ashes should be:

  ☐ Kept by family

  ☐ Scattered at: _____

  ☐ Buried/interred at: _____

  ☐ Divided among: _____

Donation to Science (if preapproved):

- Organization contacted: _____
- Contact info: _____

Funeral / Memorial Service Wishes:

☐ I would like a more traditional funeral service with casket

☐ I prefer a memorial/celebration of life after cremation

☐ I don't want a service

☐ Let my family decide

Details I'd like included (songs, readings, location, speakers, etc.):

_____

_____

_____

Obituary Notes (optional):

Names to include, life highlights, how I want to be remembered, etc.

_____

_____

_____

Funeral Home (if pre-arranged):

Name: _____

Phone: _____

Contact Person: _____

Important Documents

What You Should Know

When someone dies, one of the first things families do is go looking for papers. Wills. Insurance policies. Titles. Passwords. Anything that tells them what needs to happen next.

If this information isn't clearly laid out, your family could spend days or weeks trying to piece everything together. That means added stress, delays in settling your estate, and sometimes missed benefits or financial penalties.

This section is where you point to the **documents that matter most**, and more importantly where to find them. Not just what they are, but *where they're stored.* Fireproof safe? Bottom desk drawer? Password-protected folder on your laptop? Don't assume people will know.

You don't need to attach every document here (though you can if you want). This is about creating a **map to the paperwork** that matters, so your people aren't left guessing.

If something doesn't apply to you, cross it out. If it's in progress, note that too. The goal here is clarity.

Important Documents

Document Type	Do I Have It?	Location/Notes
Last Will and Testament	☐ Yes ☐ No	
Living Trust	☐ Yes ☐ No	
Medical DPOA	☐ Yes ☐ No	
Advance Directives	☐ Yes ☐ No	
HIPAA Authorization	☐ Yes ☐ No	
Military Discharge (DD-214)	☐ Yes ☐ No	
Life Insurance Policy	☐ Yes ☐ No	
Property Deeds/Mortgage	☐ Yes ☐ No	
Vehicle Titles	☐ Yes ☐ No	
Marriage Certificate	☐ Yes ☐ No	
Divorce Decree	☐ Yes ☐ No	
Birth Certificate	☐ Yes ☐ No	
Social Security Card	☐ Yes ☐ No	
Passport/ID	☐ Yes ☐ No	
Financial Power of Attorney	☐ Yes ☐ No	
Prepaid Funeral Plan	☐ Yes ☐ No	
Safe Deposit Box/Key Info	☐ Yes ☐ No	
Tax Returns (last 2-3 years)	☐ Yes ☐ No	

Digital Access Reference

What You Should Know

Not everything important lives in a file cabinet anymore. These days, a lot of what matters like financial accounts, wills, insurance policies, even photos is stored online, behind usernames and passwords.

That's fine when you're alive and handling it. But when you're gone, **someone else needs a way in**.
And the truth is, most people have more digital accounts than they realize:

- Multiple email addresses (Gmail, Yahoo, work emails)
- Bank accounts at different banks
- Retirement plans at old jobs
- Cloud storage full of family photos
- Subscription services that keep charging monthly

This section is where you **give a roadmap to your digital world.** You don't have to list every password here (and you probably shouldn't for security reasons). But you *do* want to make sure the people handling your affairs know:

- What accounts exist
- What's stored where
- How to find the passwords, if needed

If you use a password manager (like LastPass, Bitwarden, or Dashlane), great. Make sure someone knows how to access it or at least knows where to find the master password if you're no longer here to tell them.

If you have multiple bank accounts, savings apps, or investment platforms, list them separately. Same with multiple email addresses; sometimes that's where billing notices, tax info, or insurance reminders show up.

The goal isn't to dump your entire online life here.
The goal is to give someone **enough information** that they can close accounts, protect your identity, and claim what's yours without weeks of digging and dead-end password resets.

Digital Access Reference

Type of Account	Basic Account Info	Who Can Access/ Where to Find Password
Primary Email Account	_____ _____	_____ _____
Secondary / Old Email Accounts	_____ _____	_____ _____
Cloud Storage (Dropbox, OneDrive, iCloud)	_____ _____	_____ _____
Google Drive (if separate)	_____ _____	_____ _____
Personal Computer / Laptop	_____ _____	_____ _____
Phone Unlock/Pincode	_____ _____	_____ _____
Password Manager (LastPass, Bitwarden, etc.)	_____ _____	_____ _____
Primary Bank Account	_____ _____	_____ _____
Secondary Bank / Credit Union Account	_____ _____	_____ _____
Online Retirement Account (401(k), IRA)	_____ _____	_____ _____

Type of Account	Basic Account Info	Who Can Access/ Where to Find Password
Investment / Crypto Accounts (Robinhood, Coinbase, etc.)		
Mortgage Portal / Home Loan Servicer		
Online Payment Services (PayPal, Venmo, Zelle)		
Utility Accounts (Electric, Gas, Water, Internet)		
Social Media Accounts (Facebook, Instagram, Twitter)		
Online Subscription Services (Netflix, Amazon, Spotify)		
Phone Carrier / Mobile Account		
Other Important Accounts (list below):		

Accounts and Assets

What You Should Know

After someone dies, one of the biggest questions their family faces is:

"What did they own and what do we do with it?"

Bank accounts, retirement plans, investments, life insurance, vehicles, property; it all needs to be claimed, closed, or passed on. And if nobody knows what's out there, it can lead to major delays, lost money, or even assets getting turned over to the state (it's called "escheatment" and it happens more often than you'd think).

This section gives your family a **starting point.**

You don't have to list every penny in every account. Just tell them what exists and where to find it. Whether it's a savings account at the local credit union or a 401(k) from a job you left ten years ago.

If you have updated beneficiaries listed on your accounts (which you should), many assets can skip probate and go straight to the people you chose. But they can't claim it if they don't know it's there.

Use this space to create a map.
You're not showing off what you built. You're making sure it ends up where you wanted it to go.

Accounts and Assets

Account / Asset	Institution / Location	Account Type / Asset Description
Checking Account	_____ _____	_____ _____
Savings Account	_____ _____	_____ _____
Retirement Account (401k, IRA)	_____ _____	_____ _____
Life Insurance Policy	_____ _____	_____ _____
Investment / Brokerage Account	_____ _____	_____ _____
Cryptocurrency Wallet	_____ _____	_____ _____
Home / Real Estate Property	_____ _____	_____ _____
Vehicles (cars, motorcycles, boats)	_____ _____	_____ _____
Safe Deposit Box	_____ _____	_____ _____

Account / Asset	Institution / Location	Account Type / Asset Description
Other:	_____	_____
_____	_____	_____
Other:	_____	_____
_____	_____	_____
Other:	_____	_____
_____	_____	_____
Other:	_____	_____
_____	_____	_____

Accounts and Assets

61

Military Service and VA Benefits

What You Should Know

If you served in the military, there are benefits your service earned and your family may be eligible for them when you pass. But these benefits don't show up automatically. The VA, funeral homes, and national cemeteries require proof of service, and that usually means one document: the **DD-214** (your military discharge papers).

Without that form, your family might miss out on:
- Burial in a national cemetery
- A military headstone or marker
- A folded American flag presented at your service
- Taps played at your funeral
- Financial help with burial costs
- Survivor and dependent benefits

This page is here to make sure your service isn't overlooked and that your family has what they need to honor it properly.

If you've already secured your benefits or planned for a military burial, use this space to write it down. If not, now's the time to track down your paperwork and make sure it's stored somewhere safe but accessible.

Military Service Record

Detail	Info
Branch	_____
Service Dates (Start-End)	_____
Rank at Discharge	_____
Type of Discharge	_____
Location of DD-214	_____
Enrolled in VA Healthcare?	☐ Yes ☐ No ☐ Unsure

VA Burial Benefits Checklist

☐ I want to be buried in a national or state veterans cemetery

☐ My DD-214 is on file or included in this planner

☐ I want military honors at my service (flag, Taps, etc.)

☐ I've discussed my wishes with my family or executor

☐ I've applied for pre-need eligibility with the VA

Notes or Special Instructions

_____

_____

_____

✎ Quick Link: VA Pre-Need Burial Eligibility

Want to make things easier for your family? You can apply for burial benefits now, while you're alive, and have your eligibility confirmed in advance.

Apply here:

🔗 https://www.va.gov/burials-memorials/pre-need-eligibility

Letters to Loved Ones

What You Should Know

This section is about the heart, not paperwork.

These aren't legal forms. There's no right way to write them. These are your words; meant for the people who meant the most to you.

Maybe you want to say thank you. Maybe you want to share a memory, pass down advice, or offer a little comfort when things get hard. Maybe you just want someone to know that they mattered.

You don't have to write all the letters now. You don't have to get poetic. You just have to be honest.

If you're not ready to write anything here, that's okay too. Use this space to jot down ideas. Write a note. Leave a voice memo. Attach something handwritten. Whatever helps you say what you'd want to say if you didn't get the chance later.

And if you've already written a letter?
Perfect. Tuck it in here and make a note of who it's for.

This is your voice, even after you're gone.
Give it to the people who need to hear it.

Optional Writing Prompts

You don't have to be a writer. You just have to be honest.
Choose one that speaks to you or answer them all.

If I Had One More Minute With You, I'd Say...

_____
_____
_____
_____
_____
_____
_____
_____
_____

Here's What I Always Wanted You to Know...

_____
_____
_____
_____
_____
_____
_____
_____

This Is What I Loved Most About You...

_____

_____

_____

_____

_____

What I Hope You Remember About Me...

_____

_____

_____

_____

_____

Advice I'd Want You to Carry With You...

_____

_____

_____

_____

_____

_____

_____

_____

Blank Letter Pages

To: _____

_____
_____
_____
_____
_____
_____
_____
_____
_____

To: _____

_____
_____
_____
_____
_____
_____
_____
_____
_____
_____

To: _____

_____

_____

_____

_____

_____

_____

_____

_____

To: _____

_____

_____

_____

_____

_____

_____

_____

_____

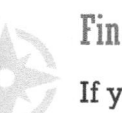

Final Thoughts

If you made it this far, then let me be the first to say it:
You've already done more than most people ever do.

You've taken on some hard questions. You've made decisions your family won't have to make in the dark. You've created something that will guide them when you can't. That's not easy. But it's one of the most loving things a person can do.

This planner isn't about being morbid.
It's about making chaos just a little less chaotic.
It's about giving people answers instead of anxiety.
And it's about making sure your voice still carries—even when you're not in the room.

You don't have to fill this all out in one sitting.
You don't have to do it perfectly.
Just keep showing up, one page at a time. Come back to it when life changes. Leave notes in the margins. Scribble stuff out. Make it yours.

And when the time comes, whether it's expected or not, this planner becomes a gift.
Not just a binder full of documents, but a roadmap.
A north star.

So thank you for taking this seriously.
For preparing. For protecting your people.
For making something that matters.

You did good.

 - **Ben**

Appendix A

This appendix provides a quick reference for legal execution requirements by state for three common healthcare planning documents:

- Advance Directives
- Durable Power of Attorney for Healthcare (DPOA)
- Mental Health Directives (where applicable)

Each state may have specific rules regarding witness signatures, notarization, or both. Always verify with your state's most current statutes or consult a legal professional for the most accurate and enforceable forms.

State/Territory	Advance Directive	DPOA	Mental Health Directive
Alabama	2 Witnesses	2 Witnesses	Not Specified
Alaska	2 Witnesses or Notary	2 Witnesses or Notary	Not Specified
Arizona	2 Witnesses or Notary	2 Witnesses	2 Witnesses
Arkansas	2 Witnesses	2 Witnesses	Not Specified
California	2 Witnesses or Notary	2 Witnesses or Notary	2 Witnesses
Colorado	2 Witnesses or Notary	2 Witnesses	2 Witnesses
Connecticut	2 Witnesses	2 Witnesses	Not Specified
Delaware	2 Witnesses or Notary	2 Witnesses	Not Specified
Florida	2 Witnesses	2 Witnesses	2 Witnesses
Georgia	2 Witnesses	2 Witnesses	Notary
Hawaii	2 Witnesses or Notary	2 Witnesses	Not Specified
Idaho	Notary	Notary	Not Specified
Illinois	1 Witness	1 Witness	2 Witnesses
Indiana	2 Witnesses	2 Witnesses	Notary
Iowa	2 Witnesses or Notary	2 Witnesses	Not Specified

Kansas	2 Witnesses or Notary	2 Witnesses	2 Witnesses
Kentucky	2 Witnesses or Notary	Notary	Not Specified
Louisiana	2 Witnesses	2 Witnesses	Not Specified
Maine	2 Witnesses	2 Witnesses	Not Specified
Maryland	2 Witnesses	2 Witnesses	2 Witnesses
Massachusetts	2 Witnesses	2 Witnesses	Not Specified
Michigan	2 Witnesses	2 Witnesses	Not Specified
Minnesota	2 Witnesses or Notary	2 Witnesses	2 Witnesses
Mississippi	2 Witnesses	2 Witnesses	Not Specified
Missouri	2 Witnesses	2 Witnesses	Not Specified
Montana	Notary	Notary	Not Specified
Nebraska	2 Witnesses	2 Witnesses	Not Specified
Nevada	2 Witnesses	2 Witnesses	Notary
New Hampshire	Notary	Notary	Not Specified
New Jersey	2 Witnesses	2 Witnesses	Not Specified
New Mexico	2 Witnesses	2 Witnesses	2 Witnesses
New York	2 Witnesses	2 Witnesses	Not Specified
North Carolina	2 Witnesses and Notary	Notary	2 Witnesses
North Dakota	2 Witnesses or Notary	2 Witnesses	Not Specified
Ohio	2 Witnesses or Notary	2 Witnesses or Notary	Notary
Oklahoma	2 Witnesses	2 Witnesses	Not Specified
Oregon	2 Witnesses or Notary	2 Witnesses or Notary	2 Witnesses
Pennsylvania	2 Witnesses	2 Witnesses	Not Specified
Rhode Island	2 Witnesses	2 Witnesses	Not Specified
South Carolina	2 Witnesses	2 Witnesses	Not Specified
South Dakota	2 Witnesses	2 Witnesses	Not Specified
Tennessee	2 Witnesses or Notary	2 Witnesses	Not Specified
Texas	2 Witnesses or Notary	Notary	Notary
Utah	Notary	Notary	Notary
Vermont	2 Witnesses or Notary	2 Witnesses or Notary	Not Specified
Virginia	2 Witnesses	2 Witnesses	2 Witnesses

Washington	2 Witnesses	2 Witnesses	2 Witnesses
West Virginia	2 Witnesses or Notary	2 Witnesses or Notary	2 Witnesses
Wisconsin	2 Witnesses	2 Witnesses	Not Specified
Wyoming	2 Witnesses	2 Witnesses	Not Specified
District of Columbia	2 Witnesses	2 Witnesses	Not Specified
Puerto Rico	2 Witnesses or Notary	Notary	Not Specified
Guam	2 Witnesses	2 Witnesses	Not Specified
U.S. Virgin Islands	2 Witnesses	2 Witnesses	Not Specified
American Samoa	2 Witnesses	2 Witnesses	Not Specified
Northern Mariana Islands	2 Witnesses	2 Witnesses	Not Specified

Made in the USA
Monee, IL
23 August 2025

22860486R00044